MASTERS AND CHAMPIONS
CLASSICAL GREECE:
300 YEARS OF BRITISH INSPIRATION

5th to 3rd Century BC Greek Sculpture and 19th Century British Drawings and Paintings
from The British Museum and The Collection of Lord Elgin

9 June 2012 - 26 August 2012

ISBN No 978-0-9565234-1-9

Published by Moray Art Centre

Copyright © Moray Art Centre

2012, Moray Art Centre, Findhorn, Scotland, UK

Supported by:
Creative Scotland
Big Lottery
Highlands and Islands Enterprise

Granted the Inspire mark, the badge
of the London 2012 Inspire programme.

CONTENTS

Drawing of the Parthenon frieze,
by Feodor Ivanovitch, from portfolio: Elgin Drawings Vol. 4.
© The Trustees of the British Museum

FOREWORD

Mr Neil MacGregor, OM, Director, The British Museum

I am delighted that the Partnership UK scheme has once more brought together the British Museum and Moray Art Centre, our most northerly British partner. Masters and Champions is a beautiful and fascinating exhibition that eloquently connects the Scottish Enlightenment of the 18th and early 19th centuries with the Golden Age of 5th-century BC Athens. Choosing an exhibition for the Olympic summer of 2012 Moray Art Centre has taken inspiration from Ancient Greece, the original home of the Games. In particular, the exhibition focuses on the horse in Greek art, life and myth with particular reference to the incomparable horses of the Parthenon Sculptures.

The Ancient Greeks produced some of the most spirited images of the horse that the world has ever seen. The head of the Horse of Selene, from the east pediment of the Parthenon, for example, is designed and carved with consummate skill. Greek sculptors excelled in turning cold marble into warm flesh, but Selene's Horse is no mere petrification of a living creature, no mere portrait of one individual horse. Rather, in this beast, exhausted by the effort of drawing a chariot of the moon goddess across the dark sky, the sculptor has captured the very essence of his subject.

The Horse of Selene is represented in the exhibition by a cast from Broomhall, the house built by Thomas Bruce, 7th Earl of Elgin. The present Earl has, himself, generously become a partner in the creation of this exhibition, both as provider of loans and also as contributor to the accompanying catalogue. Sharing its collection is a primary purpose of the British Museum and, when the borrower makes such good use of material as that seen in the Moray Art Centre, I feel a double sense of pride. Long may our happy relationship continue! ■

A GOLDEN AGE

Randy Klinger, Founder and Director, Moray Art Centre

As far as we know, the first time that our species has ever made a deliberate and concerted effort to realistically portray nature in a systematic development was in ancient Greece during an approximate 200-year period, or barely six generations. As a point of comparison, the works of their predecessors, the Egyptians, saw a modest evolution of their nearly 5,000 year civilisation.

Professor Ernst Gombrich, wrote, 'What makes it [Greek art] unique is precisely the directed efforts, the continued and systematic modifications of the schemata of conceptual art, till making was replaced by the matching of reality through the new skill of mimesis.' *

The premise of this exhibition is to pose a question: As we look at the manifestations of the minds, talents and impulses of 5th-century BC Greece, with their revolutionary development of philosophical thought and aesthetic ambition, what would it take to generate a Golden Age in our own time?

How could our culture 'magnetise' all the necessary minds, find a focus of shared intention, and incubate the wealth of skills and clarity of perception needed to distil shared cultural criteria that could birth the next Golden Age? What could this Golden Age look like? Or does the current populace believe that, in an age of such diversity and relativity of criteria, a shared, unified goal is now impossible?

We wish to extend our very deepest gratitude and appreciation to The Trustees, Director and Heads of Greece and Rome, Paintings and Prints and Drawings of The British Museum, and to Lord and Lady Elgin for making this exhibition possible.

We would especially like to express our gratitude to The British Museum:

- Neil MacGregor OM, Director
- Dr Andrew Burnett FBA CBE, Deputy Director
- Dr Ian Jenkins, OBE FSA, Senior Curator,
  Department of Greece and Rome
- John Orna Ornstein,
  Head of London and National Programmes
- Lesley Fitton, The Keeper, Department of Greece and Rome
- Hugo Chapman, The Keeper,
  Department of Prints and Drawings
- Andrew Bashan, Senior Administrator and Loans Registrar,
  Prints and Drawings
- Trevor Coughlan, Senior Administrator,
  Department of Greece and Rome
- Celeste Farge, Curator of Drawings,
  Department of Greece and Rome
- Alex Truscott, Senior Museum Assistant,
  Department of Greece and Rome

We extend our profound gratitude and appreciation to Lord and Lady Elgin for kindly loaning important works of art from their collection and for their vast knowledge, insight and authority, offering a unique link to 19th century history.

We would like to thank Professor Elizabeth Moignard, who brought her expertise and scholarship to this exhibition, and Dr Ian Jenkins, who generously shared his vast knowledge, time and perspicacity and without whose partnership this exhibition could not have happened.

We give special appreciation to The Big Lottery, Creative Scotland and Highlands and Islands Enterprise Moray, whose generous support made this exhibition and associated events possible. ∎

* Gombrich, E.H. (1996) *Art and Illusion*,
  'Reflections on the Greek Revolution',
  London: Phaidon.

Drawing of the Parthenon frieze,
by Feodor Ivanovitch, from portfolio: Elgin Drawings Vol. 4.
© The Trustees of the British Museum

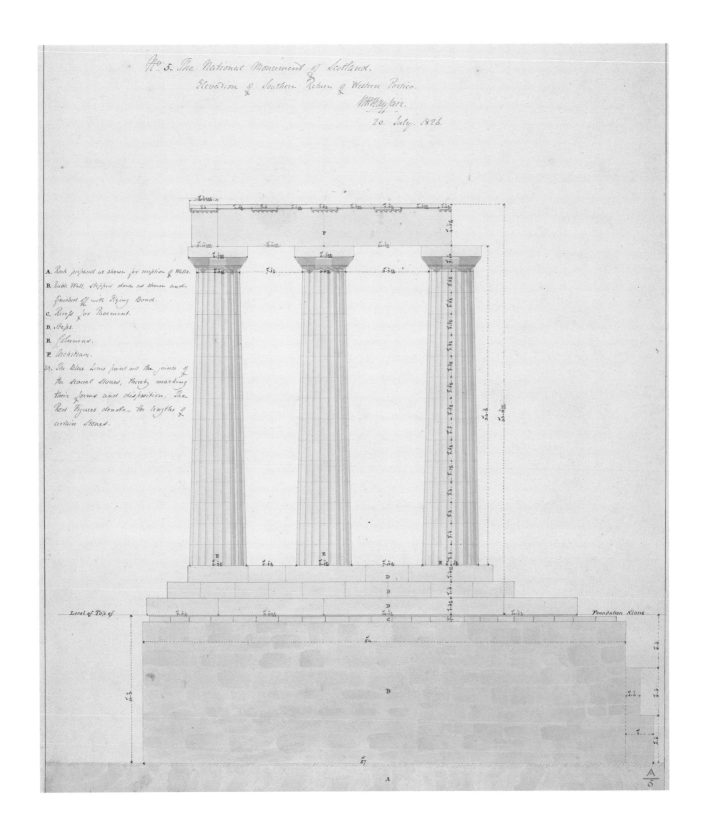

ATHENIANS OF THE NORTH

Dr Ian Jenkins, OBE FSA, Senior Curator,
Department of Greece and Rome, The British Museum

'She certainly is a whapper', remarked Lady Elgin of Lady Emma Hamilton when, in autumn 1799, she and Thomas Bruce, 7th Earl of Elgin, stopped off at Sicily on the way to Istanbul. The Earl and Countess were excited at the prospect of a new adventure, for Elgin had just been despatched as British ambassador to the court of the Ottoman Sultan, Selim III. Sir William Hamilton, by contrast, was nearing the end of his long sojourn in Naples where, since 1764, he had resided as Britain's diplomatic representative and, in company with his ample wife and her lover, Admiral Lord Nelson, he was on the point of departure for London.

Hamilton was descended on both sides of his family from one of Scotland's noblest families, and his great name, coupled with his diplomatic appointment, had instilled in him a sense of public duty to use his residence in a foreign land as a means of promoting the arts and manufacture at home. Hamilton was, by the time Elgin met him, famous throughout Europe as a connoisseur, and his great collection of Greek vases and many other antiquities had transformed the British Museum when it was acquired for the nation in 1772. Lord Elgin was bound by the same noblesse oblige and, even before setting out, he had begun to recruit artists and antiquaries for the purpose of recording the ancient monuments of ancient Greece.

The Scottish Enlightenment was part of a great pan-European movement that shone its light into the dark abyss of time in order to dispel superstition and illuminate the path of reason. The flame of true understanding was lit from Greek fire and, as Greek Revival architecture took root in Edinburgh, so the city would become known as 'The Athens of The North'. *

To mark the 2012 Olympics, the Moray Art Centre is showing an exhibition dedicated to Ancient Greece as seen through the eyes of three Enlightenment Scots: 7th Earl of Elgin, Thomas Bruce (1766–1841), modeller and carver, John Henning (1771–1851), and the traveller and artist, James Skene (1775–1864) of Rubislaw.

With the Olympics in mind, the exhibition looks in particular at the horse in myth, art and life. In Athenian society, the horse-owning class stood high within the social hierarchy. Youths of well-to-do families were trained from early years in the art of horsemanship in expectation of serving in the Athenian cavalry. Demonstrations of riding in formation were one of the great sights of Athens, and especially so when around 440 BC the fighting force was increased from some 300 to 1,000. The cavalry reforms were instituted by Pericles, Athens' premier statesman at the time. He also presided over the great programme of architectural renewal of his city that would create the Parthenon and other splendid buildings on the Acropolis. Pericles' new cavalry and the magnificent impression it made upon his fellow citizens is commemorated in the cavalcades of the Parthenon frieze. Ahead of these mounted horsemen in the frieze were chariot races in which four horses drew a lightweight car. In the 5th century BC the chariot was long out of use as a vehicle of war, but it continued to feature in sport and in ceremony such as in the marriage festival. In Greek myth and art it is also the conveyance in which gods and heroes travel. In the east pediment of the Parthenon, for example, the miraculous birth of Athena was framed in one corner by the sun god Helios driving his chariot horses before him as he brings the new day. In the other corner Selene, goddess of the Moon, sinks beneath the horizon, her horses exhausted by the effort of drawing her chariot across the night sky.

The survival of the head of Selene's horse, along with the other sculptures of the Parthenon is owed to the foresight and energy of 7th Earl of Elgin. In spring 1802, Elgin visited Athens for the first time. The city was then part of the Ottoman empire, and Elgin saw for himself the ongoing destruction of the sculptures of the Parthenon and other monuments. He rescued what he could of the sculptures and some pieces of architecture from the Parthenon and other Acropolis monuments and brought them back to Britain. When they first went on show in early summer 1807, the sculptures of the Parthenon made a great impact upon those who saw them. They included the artist Benjamin Robert Haydon and the Scottish modeller and carver John Henning. A Parliamentary Select Committee Enquiry was held in 1816 to establish, among other matters, Lord Elgin's entitlement to the sculptures, the sum of compensation that he should receive for his considerable financial outlay and, not least, to assess the artistic worth of the collection and its suitability as a national acquisition. The 'Elgin Marbles' have been redisplayed many times since they were first shown in the British Museum in 1817. They were thought then to be the greatest artworks known to humankind and they remain collectively one of the great treasures of the British Museum. Beautiful and fascinating in themselves, they also serve as a reminder of the Golden Age of Athens that, in the 5th century BC, saw great advances in nearly every aspect of creative endeavour. In art and architecture, in prose-writing and poetry, in the telling of history and in drama, in politics and in moral philosophy, the Greek experience was to shape our understanding of what it is to be human. In this Olympic year this exhibition is a timely reminder of the debt that we owe to the great Greek experiment in intellectual humanism. ∎

* The National Monument by C.R. Cockerell and W.H. Playfair (unfinished replica of the Parthenon, Carlton Hill, Edinburgh, 1822–1829).

THE CLASSICAL HORSE THROUGH BRITISH EYES

Professor Elizabeth A. Moignard MA DPhil FSA FRSE
Classics, University of Glasgow

The celebration of the Olympic Games in Britain in 2012, prompts, not for the first time, reflection on the nature and history of Britain's conceptual relationship with Classical Greece, and particularly with the Greece which we came to view through the arrival of original Greek artefacts in Britain in the 18th and early 19th centuries. An architectural taste pioneered earlier by Inigo Jones and enhanced later by Robert Adam provided a context for a sense of formal antiquity which supported the display of Classical sculpture, often Roman and often damaged and restored, as a yardstick for visual aspiration. Classical art, whatever its origins, came to be viewed as the outward sign of a cultural golden age; the formal proportions of Classical buildings, and the emphasis on the perfect human form, especially the young and athletic body, became an aesthetic assumption, and a sign of an ancient perfection. That sense of a golden age underlay a parallel sense of the nature of Classical Greek, and particularly Athenian society, which is arguably still with us, despite the much more nuanced scholarship which now interprets its remains, textual and physical, as representatives of a culture whose imperfections are in themselves as important as its positive achievements. Furthermore, The Queen's Diamond Jubilee, celebrated during the same few weeks, provides an added spur, to thoughts about our national sense of self and aspiration, our concepts of perfection, and the nature of a golden age, or a cultural climax.

Greece and its surviving Classical artefacts gradually grew better known in Britain during the 18th century, as the country itself began to emerge from political obscurity as part of the Ottoman empire, and grand tourists and inquisitive antiquarians began to visit and report on what they saw, with a view to understanding its history. Lord Elgin's own expedition which culminated in the acquisition of the 'Marbles' came, in some senses, towards the end of this particular voyage of discovery; his use of draughtsmen and cast makers sits in the tradition of exploratory reporting already established by Stuart and Revett*, among others. After the marbles, casts and drawings made in situ arrived in Britain, they became a focus and an inspiration for artists, John Henning and Benjamin Robert Haydon among them.

Their drawings are themselves powerful indicators of the use of their graphic skills as a tool for rather more than illustrative reportage: they explore, reconstruct, and improve on what they were seeing. Their work parallels a fierce contemporary debate about what the editors of ancient texts were doing: was it their function to report what actually survived, to restore what might have been there originally, or to improve on it?

The Parthenon sculptures acquired by Lord Elgin were first displayed in London in a temporary gallery in Piccadilly and eventually, after the British government decided to acquire them, in the British Museum, in 1817. Their separation from their parent building is, in itself, perhaps an under-emphasised factor in their reception as art by the contemporary viewer. The ancient viewer, we should remember, had much less opportunity to look at them closely: on the building they were out of reach, and seen at a considerable distance and often at a manipulated angle. The history of the Parthenon as a romantic ruin, and as a type-site for the study of Classical architecture tends to place emphasis on the building, despite the drawings of Jacques Carrey (1674), and of William Pars for Stuart and Revett's publication, which are as illustrative of the sculptures as of their supporting building.

The implications of the drawings by Charles Robert Cockerell and Benjamin Robert Haydon of the original display are a dissociation of the art from the structure, and perhaps even more noticeably, an assimilation of the frieze sculptures towards a status as flat art – something comparable with a painting, rather than a three-dimensional object. They could be viewed as art rather than objects, and separated from the implications of decorative and tactile qualities which would have placed them further down the generally accepted hierarchy of artistic importance and quality. It is still arguable that the current display in the Duveen Gallery of the British Museum places emphasis on the frieze viewed as a strip image, and on the *metopes*, more than on the pedimental sculptures, and not entirely as a consequence of the greater number of reliefs in the collection. Furthermore, the dissemination of the frieze, in particular, as casts to art

---

* Stuart, J.& Revett, N. (1762–1816) *The antiquities of Athens and other monuments of Greece.* London.

The Measurement of The Marble,
with the Number _____ Porphyry

at Mr Grindeys Westminster
No 1 a great Jamb
2 a Column 9 feet 6 by 2 feet 3
3 a Do 5 feet 6 by 2 feet 2
4 a Do 4 feet by 2 feet
5 a Do 4 feet 4 by 2 feet 1
6 a Do 4 feet 4 by 2 feet
7 a Do 5 feet 4 by 2 feet
8 a Do 4 feet 4 by 2 feet

In the Museum   Porphyry
No 1 a Column 3 feet 6 by 1 foot 3

                    Parian
No 1 a Column 4 feet 10 by 1 foot 6

                In the yard
No 1 a Column 7 feet by 1 foot 3
2 a Do 5 feet 2 by 2 feet
3 a Do 4 feet 2 by 2 feet
4 a Do 4 feet 2 by 2 feet
5 a Do 6 feet by 1 foot 3

        Verd antique
No 1 a Column 4 feet by 1 foot 4
2 a Do 4 feet by 1 foot 2
                    Carrd over

List of decorative marble, written in the hand of Thomas,
7th Earl of Elgin.

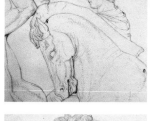

schools and for incorporation into local government buildings up and down Britain during the 19th century enhanced its status as a great work of art in its own right. This view was vigorously enhanced by connoisseurs of antiquity, including Charles Newton, for whom it represented a gold standard in the development of ancient art towards a state of perfection. The continued educational use of the display in the British Museum for drawing embedded a sense of the sculptures as a yardstick in the history of figurative art.

The exhibition concentrates on another interesting, and in a British context, particularly appealing feature of the marbles – their association of the human interest with the horse. A large proportion of the frieze in London depicts a section of a procession which is mounted and moving, or the preparation for riding; the horses are treated with the same degree of observation and interest as the human figures. Furthermore, the head of Selene's horse from the corner of the east pediment is an equally dramatic and sympathetic portrayal of the triumphant exhaustion of an animal as dear to the British psyche as to that of the ancient Athenian. For both, the horse is transport and an agent of movement and travel, a sign of status, an embodiment of competitive beauty, and a generator of enormous emotional commitment.

The presence of the riders in the Parthenon frieze is, in itself, a source of academic enquiry. It is usually assumed that the procession is an ideal version of a real and iterative event in Athenian public life: the Panathenaic procession, which paraded a newly woven dress for Athena en route to the Acropolis for presentation to her cult statue. This handover is the central feature of the east frieze, not altogether

observed with attention by the Olympian gods. Argument persists about the ideological intentions of this particular portrait of the event, which is often assumed not to have involved cavalry in real life, although it did include men of military age. There is an essential consensus on the status of the Parthenon and its sculptures as a key expression of Athenian identity for Athenian citizens: it was built under the direction of Pericles with funds originally assembled for defence, provided employment for a large number of people, and expressed a sense of self for Athens at a time of widespread conflict. The incorporation of a representation of its primary celebration of that self into the structure carries a striking message. The inclusion of the horsemen has been interpreted variously, perhaps most recently as a marker of Pericles' active encouragement of cavalry in terms of numbers and status as a key feature of citizen responsibility. This sits tellingly alongside the presentation of the athletic male body; fitness is a key factor in military capability – here, as elsewhere in Athenian visual art, it becomes both an aesthetic desirable and an indicator of status. Competitive athletics enjoyed a high social status precisely because they underwrote the capability of a citizen army.

The horse occupies a parallel position in ancient Greek culture to its status in ours: an animal whose value as a transport mechanism was historically undisputed, but whose care and employment was expensive, particularly when employed as a chariot team, or as a potentially expendable mount in military activity. It is interesting to notice a current upsurge in emotional interest in the history of this relationship surrounding the dramatisation and the film of the book *War Horse*. The association of the horse with high status, with display, competition, and also with heroism is noticeably present in ancient Greek art, just as it was in British art of the 18th and 19th centuries. Stubbs' painting *Whistlejacket* is perhaps the embodiment of a cultural sense of the horse as a heroic presence in its own right, in a Britain which had adopted equine sports, including racing, as a national passion, not just as the primarily aristocratic sport it had once been. By the time the Parthenon sculptures arrived in London, they were speaking to the converted: their emphasis on the beauty and competitive spirit of both horses and humans won wide admiration.

This exhibition foregrounds the portrayal of the horse in that context by the ancient Greek artist, and some of the agents of their dissemination in Britain. Ancient Greek vases have been a focus of collecting activity in Europe since the Renaissance, and were quite as powerful a disseminator of a sense of the culture which produced them as sculpture. Herakles was a key hero for the original viewers of the black figure amphora in this exhibition – a group of receptive potential and actual athletes and soldiers at a symposium. Herakles had a difficult and exhausting career, with many opponents to overcome and many mistakes to survive. He did survive, and was eventually received in Olympus to become a god. The amphora shows him fighting Geryon: he won. The other side of the vase shows a wheeling chariot, a picture full of energy and movement. The message is one of effort, competition and reward. It is also of romance and aspiration.

Other three-dimensional exhibits include a sensitive study of a horse-head in marble, part of a sculpture probably made about a century later than the Parthenon sculpture of Selene's horse-head, shown in this exhibition as a cast loaned by Lord Elgin, with which it makes an interesting comparison. Also shown is a relief sculpture of an excited chariot team, perhaps made in Athens as a thank-offering for victory in a race.

The Elgin Throne, now in the Getty Museum, appears here as a cast lent by Lord Elgin. The original is often reported and understood as the official chair of a dignitary presiding over ceremonies, competitive sport among them. Its relief sculptures portray two episodes, one mythical, and one at least partially historical, which were central to the Athenian sense of identity: Theseus, the king of a legendary Athens, repelling an Amazon invasion, and the Tyrannicides who were credited with the birth of democracy. Theseus appears again in one of John Henning's drawings of a *metope* from the temple of Hephaistos, once again winning a fight.

The reception and wider publication of the Parthenon sculptures provides another thread in this exhibition's exploratory tapestry. The drawings made by John Henning of both casts and original sculptures eventually generated, among other things, a set of miniature casts of the Parthenon frieze: Lord Elgin's set of these appears in this exhibition. As important, however, are a selection of the drawings themselves: a portfolio of Henning's work remains in the Elgin collection, and some of them are exhibited for the first time. All but one of the drawings of the frieze feature parts of the west section, which actually remained on the Parthenon until 1993: they were made from the casts, and with reference to earlier drawings made in situ. There are also some studies of divine figures from the pediments, which Henning saw on display. There is an interesting comparison to be made between these and the Haydon drawings loaned both by Lord Elgin and by the British Museum. The Cockerell and Haydon drawings offer an invaluable insight into the effect and impact of the original exhibition.

They also underline a quality of observation of both the human and of the horse which supports our expression of interest in the celebration, ancient and modern, of the relationship between the two, empathetic, competitive, and aesthetic, in the context of prestigious events which do the same. ∎

A PERSONAL REFLECTION

Lord Elgin, The Earl of Elgin and Kincardine, KT

Early in 1799, Thomas, 7th Earl of Elgin returned to Scotland after serving as Envoy Extraordinary in Berlin since 1795. He married, on 11th March 1799, Mary, the only child of William Hamilton Nisbet of Dirleton. With his bride he discussed further improvements to be made at Broomhall, his family seat in Fife. The architect, Thomas Harrison, also suggested that Elgin, having been appointed Ambassador to the Ottoman Empire at Constantinople, should take a team of artists to work in Greece and that it would be of enormous value if moulds could be made of the important buildings, especially in Athens. Casts made from such moulds would enable architects to achieve the perfection so characteristic of ancient Greek architecture.

Alas, the British Government were unresponsive and it was not until Elgin reached Palermo and there met Sir William Hamilton that a team was formed under the leadership of Giovanni Battista Lusieri. Elgin told Lusieri that there would be at least an artist to paint figures and another to make moulds. However, the party eventually consisted of Vincenzo Ballestra and his companion Sebastian Ittar, each highly competent architects; Feodor Ivanovitch, draughtsman of figures and sculpture, Bernardino Ledus and Vincenzo Rosati, both *formatori* or moulders for casts and, of course, Lusieri himself, whose brilliant landscapes in water colour are today hugely admired.

After inevitable travel problems, owing to adverse wind, the party reached Athens on 22nd July 1800 and there, in the main, they were to stay for two and a half years.

Since it is more relevant for this exhibition to tell the story of the making of the moulds, I will concentrate on this accordingly. The *formatori* completed:

- The entire frieze of the Monument of Lysicrates
- The whole of the west side of the Parthenon frieze
- The best preserved portions of the north side of the Parthenon
- Two *metopes* of the Parthenon
- The bust of a Caryatid
- Much of the ornament of the portico of the Erectheum
- The whole frieze of the Theseum (east side) and almost all of the west side, together with four *metopes*

Their working conditions were hazardous; long wooden step ladders led to a narrow wooden platform hung by ropes from the walls of buildings such as the Parthenon – every scrap of their gypsum and water laboriously carried to them by oxen. More often than not, intense heat surrounded them, and they had to be careful to not unduly overlook the inhabitants of the miscellany of dwellings below them.

The cases containing the moulds were conveyed to Plymouth by Captain Stephenson, commanding the Diana frigate, to whom Elgin sent a covering letter in which he described the moulds 'as perhaps the most important things ever to be sent to Britain …' Bit by bit, the crates containing both the moulds and the actual sculptures reached the southern ports of England. Because Lord and Lady Elgin, on their return journey from Constantinople, had been detained in France on the outbreak of war in 1804, the Dowager Countess of Elgin found herself responsible for dealing with the Customs and then obtaining a safe repository.

In this role, the Dowager was fortunate in having a most distinguished private circle of noble ladies, including two duchesses, who persuaded their husbands to offer lodging for the considerable number of packing cases arriving by sea.

However, by 1807, after his return from captivity in France, Elgin had taken a lease of a house and a garden in Park Lane. Here William Porden designed a simple pitched roof building with large roof lights and so, for the first time, the collection was displayed and available to be seen and enjoyed and, before long, became a place of pilgrimage. Benjamin Robert Haydon's comments may be considered typical. He remembers being in the throes of anxiety over a painting commissioned by Lord Mulgrave, when David Wilkie called and proposed that they should go to Park Lane and see the 'Elgin Marbles'. When they arrived, Haydon later wrote – 'We walked in with the utmost nonchalance' – but not for long! – his skilful eye soon spotted the wrist of a figure so beautifully composed that he was instantly enraptured. He later wrote 'I remember thinking that they would at last rouse the art of Europe from its slumber.'

As the 19th century advanced, demand from Italy, France, Germany and Russia was to ensure that sets of the casts of the major pieces of the collection became widely desirable. Even in the United States a significant surge of interest arose. In Britain, another opportunity of interested delight came from the energetic nimble-fingered John Henning. His family had long been settled in Paisley where they helped to create the intricate designs required by the looms on which the Paisley patterned fabrics were woven. Henning had also successfully made a reputation for his miniature portrait cameos. He proposed to Elgin that he should be allowed access to the Park Lane gallery, in order to draw the marbles and then reconstitute missing heads and limbs before setting all in moulds, from which to take, in various sizes, perfect examples of the Collection. This he achieved and thus, if required, one could own in plaster miniature the entire triumphal scenes from the frieze of the Parthenon.

Since this is the year when the Olympic Games are to be held in London, I suggested that the cast of one of the Judgement Thrones for the Games in 412 BC might kindle interest. The original throne was presented to Lord Elgin on his visit to Athens in 1802 by the Archbishop of Athens. Hence you can feel something of what must have been a truly rich, though simple, grandeur which presided over the events of 2,600 years ago.

As Thomas Harrison so truly remarked to my ancestor, it is from seeing something in-the-round that really gives the thrill of absolute truth; I wish you all well in such enjoyment. ∎

Thomas, 7th Earl of Elgin's signature.

Broomhall, the ancestral home of the Elgins,
by kind permission of Mr Craig Lindsay

CATALOGUE

Image: by kind permission of Lord Elgin.

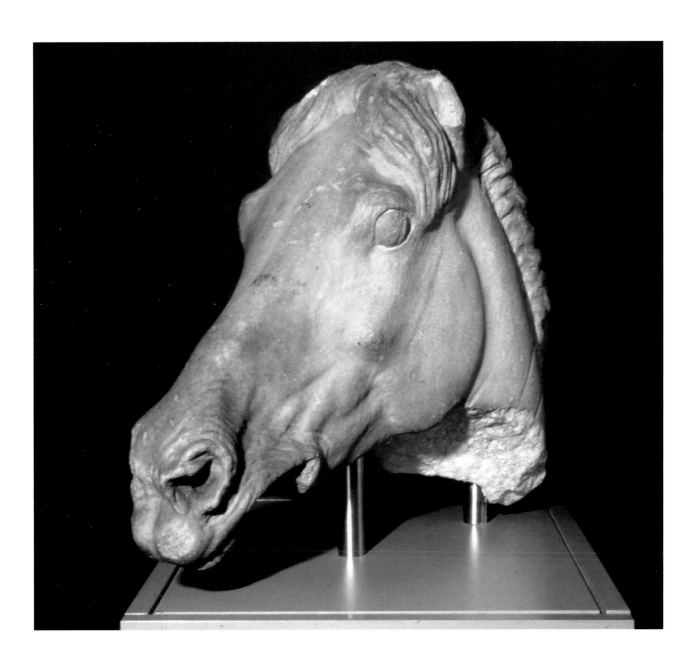

right

FRAGMENT OF A MARBLE VOTIVE RELIEF OF A RACING CHARIOT WITH FOUR HORSES GALLOPING TO LEFT (HEAD OF FURTHEST HORSE LOST)

Classical Greek, possibly carved in Athens
400–350 BC
Height: 40.5 cm (max), Width: 47 cm (max),
Depth: 10 cm (max.)

previous

MARBLE HEAD OF A HORSE TURNING BACK TO THE RIGHT, PERHAPS FROM A GROUP OF A MAN AND HIS HORSE OR FROM A CHARIOT GROUP

Western Greek, Made in Taranto
c. 350–300 BC
Height: 38 cm, Width: 59 cm, Depth: 18 cm (all approx.)

This extraordinary life-like portrait of a horse's head is one of the most sensitive representations of the animal to survive from antiquity. Its flaring nostrils, flowing mane and gaping mouth suggest that it was once part of an action figure which may have comprised a single horseman or possibly a four-horse chariot team like that represented in the Greek relief shown in this exhibition. The sculpture comes from Taranto, in southern Italy which was known as Magna Græcia (Great Greece) and which region the Greeks had colonised from earliest times. Taranto, or Tarentum as it was known in ancient times, was a great centre of sculpture modelled in clay and fired as terracotta. This head, however, is in marble from the Aegean world. There was no ready local source of the material.

This fragment of an original Greek relief-carving was once perhaps part of a commemorative monument celebrating the victory of the driver or perhaps the owner of a successful chariot in one of the festival games. The four-horse chariot or quadriga was, by the time this sculpture was made, long out of use as a vehicle of war and was used only as a ceremonial vehicle featuring in religious procession or in athletic competition. The chariot race took various forms depending on the nature of the festival, its location and the type of track. In all cases, however, the most interesting and dangerous part of any race was at the turning posts. One of the highlights of the games in Athens, the so-called Panathenaic games, was the chariot race combined with a foot-race for armed warriors. In this instance, two figures rode the chariot. One was the charioteer himself who wore a distinctively long flowing tunic, while the other was a warrior who would ride in the chariot for part of the distance and then dismount while the vehicle was still in motion. He would then run to a finishing marker bearing a shield and wearing bronze breast-plate and helmet. The event was known as the *apobates* race in reference to the armed runners and their feat of agility in leaping from the moving chariot. They are most famously shown in the race which forms part of the Parthenon frieze.

top

VIEW OF THE ACROPOLIS

Watercolour drawing by James Skene dated March 1843

James Skene of Rubislaw (1775–1864), traveller and amateur draughtsman, visited Athens in the years following the Greek War of Independence, 1821–1832. In this drawing, he captures the Acropolis in the course of being cleared of its Christian and Ottoman phases of occupation. We see the Parthenon with its north side columns partially reconstructed while the Erechtheum (left), and Propylaea (foreground) stand as un-restored ruins. Skene was an important figure in the Scottish Greek Revival. He was 'Secretary of the Board of Trustees for Manufacturers in Scotland' and was extremely active in acquiring plaster casts for the artists' Academy in Edinburgh. That institution had already received in 1827 a gift of casts from Lord Elgin himself. In the mid 1830s news reached Skene that the British Museum was casting the Parthenon Sculptures in order to make new moulds for plaster casts with which to supply a number of urgent demands. Skene's own request for a new set of casts was received warmly by the Trustees of the British Museum who appealed to the Treasury for funds to defray the cost of the casts and their transport to Edinburgh totalling £380.

bottom

THE NIKE TEMPLE RECONSTRUCTED

Watercolour drawing by James Skene dated March 1843

The Temple of Athena Nike, built in the Ionic order around 430–420 BC, occupied a rocky spur overlooking the western approach to the Acropolis. It survived until it was torn apart by the Ottomans following the Venetian siege of 1687 in order to strengthen the defences of the Acropolis. It is seen here as it looked after it was first reconstructed in 1835 after the Greek War of Independence. On the extreme right hand side of the drawing can be seen the Temple of Hephaestus, a sister temple of the Parthenon, overlooking the ancient Athenian market place or *Agora*, while the left side of the picture gives a dramatic view looking west towards the ancient harbour of the city, the Piraeus, and the Sanctuary of Demeter at Eleusis. The temple has since been twice more restored, once by Nikolaos Balanos in the middle of the 20th century, and again very recently as part of the 35-year campaign of restoration of the Acropolis monuments that was completed in 2010. Lord Elgin rescued four blocks of the sculptured frieze before the Turkish fortifications were removed after Independence when, the remaining blocks of the frieze were found and restored to the Temple. These have now all been removed from the building and are replaced by casts. Elgin's blocks are considerably better preserved than those in Athens having escaped the ill effects of acid rain.

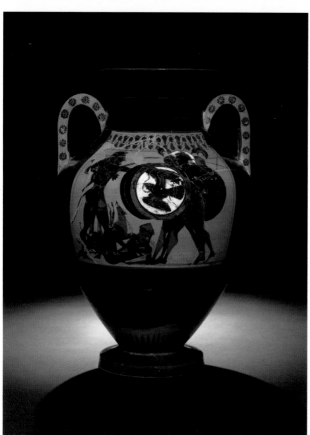

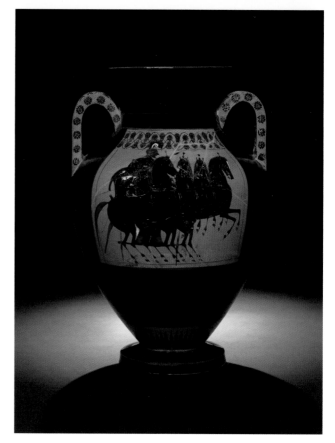

BLACK-FIGURED AMPHORA WITH DESIGNS IN BLACK ON RED PANELS WITH INTERLACING LOTUS AND HONEYSUCKLE PATTERN ABOVE; ON THE HANDLES, DOUBLE LOTUS AND HONEYSUCKLE PATTERN, BLACK, PURPLE AND WHITE; ON THE SIDES OF THE HANDLES, ROSETTES

Side a: Contest of Herakles and Geryon
Side b: *Quadriga* to front, the horses turning to right; in the car, helmeted warrior and charioteer with *pilos*, long white *chiton* and *nebris*

Amphora
Made in Athens c. 540 BC
Height: 41.3 cm, Diameter: 28 cm, Weight: 3 kg (approx)

This beautiful depiction of a four-horse war-chariot brilliantly exploits the graphic medium of black-figured vase painting. It shows a charioteer skilfully manoeuvring his team of horses into a turn on the spot. The horses' rearing foreparts are shown in a formulaic pattern that conveys the idea of movement rather than attempting to represent it realistically. The charioteer wears a tunic and worker's hat (*pilos*), and beside him is an armed warrior, the horsehair crest of whose helmet nicely answers the mane and tail of the horses themselves. The whole picture is framed within a panel of red set against the black of the body of the vessel and is flanked by the delicately painted handles. This storage amphora depicts a subject which is deliberately anachronistic since war-chariots were no longer in use in 6th century BC Athens at the time when this vase was potted and painted. The painter probably had in mind a story in Greek mythology.

TWO VIEWS OF THE HEAD OF THE HORSE OF SELENE, FROM THE EAST PEDIMENT OF THE PARTHENON, IN RIGHT PROFILE, AND A SEPARATE STUDY OF THE LEFT EYE; FORMERLY IN AN ALBUM

Black chalk, heightened with white, on blue-grey paper
Drawn by Benjamin Robert Haydon, 1809
Height: 55.6 cm, Width: 76.1 cm

Perhaps the most popular of all the sculptures to be acquired by Lord Elgin from the Parthenon in Athens is the head of a horse that once filled the corner of the east pediment. It was one of four that represented the team of horses who had spent the night drawing the chariot of the goddess of the moon Selene across the vast canopy of the night sky. However, the chariot could also be that of the dark mistress of night herself, Nyx. To balance the chariot of the sinking moon (or the waning night) in one corner of the pediment, there was, in the other corner, a representation of Helios, god of the sun, whose team was shown driven before him as they rose out of the sea at dawn. The sculptures of the Parthenon captured the imagination of the eccentrically controversial painter and teacher Benjamin Robert Haydon who, more than any of his contemporaries, acclaimed the advent of the sculptures of the Parthenon in London as a revolution in art. Haydon's powerful drawings seem to reach into the very soul of the marble creature, bringing to life the original living breathing model. Haydon was to incorporate the sculptures of the Parthenon into his own work, seeing them, as he himself put it, as a new school of art. This did not, however, make his unfashionably pompous paintings any more popular than they were, and in 1846, confronted by the failure of yet another exhibition, he tragically took his own life.

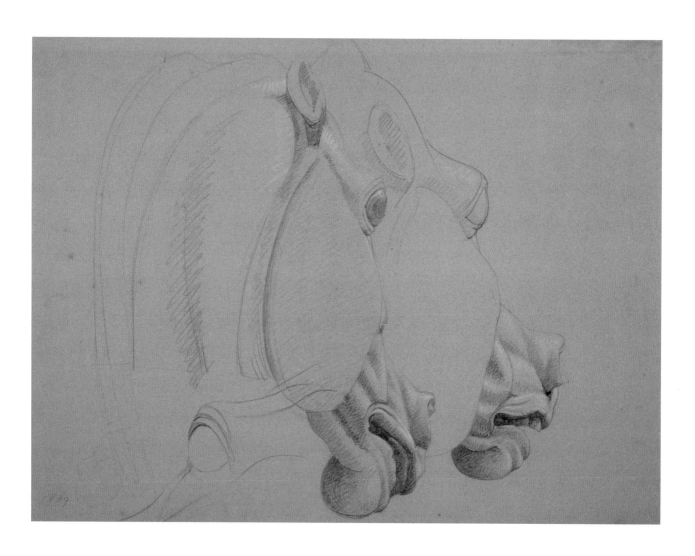

The Elgin Horses head —

Head of one of the Horses always considered to be by Lysippus — now at Venice —

It is astonishing that the great principles of Nature should have been so nearly lost in the time between Phidias & Lysippus — Compare these two heads — The Elgin head is all truth, the other all manner — In the Lysippus head the great characteristics of Nature are violated for the sake of an artificial effect, in the former head the great and inherent charac-teristics of Nature are elevated without violation — in as much as the Elgin Horses head differs from and is superior to the head by Lysippus so, do the rest of the Elgin Marbles differ from and are superior to all other Statues of this, and every subsequent age —

B. R. Haydon 1817 —

previous

STUDY OF THE HORSE'S HEAD FROM THE EAST PEDIMENT OF THE PARTHENON AND OF THE HEAD OF ONE OF THE HORSES OF ST MARK'S BASILICA, VENICE, WITH SEPARATE STUDY OF AN EYE AND EAR AT TOP RIGHT

Landseer after Haydon, etching, 1817
Height: 29.6 cm, Width: 38.8 cm

Ever pugnacious, the painter Benjamin Robert Haydon seeks to compare the marble head of a horse from the Parthenon east pediment with the head of one of the four bronze horses of St Mark's Basilica in Venice. His text asserts the marble horse to be by far superior in its observation of nature and the sheet is inscribed as follows.

'The Elgin Horses head - Head of one of the Horses always considered to be by Lysippus - now at Venice - It is astonishing that the great principles of nature should have been so nearly lost in the time between Phidias and Lysippus - compare these two heads - The Elgin head is all truth. The other all manner - In the Lysippus head the great characteristics of Nature are violated for the sake of an artificial effect, in the former head the great and inherent characteristics of nature are elevated without violation - in as much as the Elgin Horse's head differs from, and is superior to the head by Lysippus so do the rest of the 'Elgin Marbles' differ from and are superior to all other statues of this, and every subsequent age.'
B. R. Haydon 1817

The horses of St Mark's were greatly revered in the early 19th century, as they are today. Haydon is poking the art establishment in the eye by suggesting that the horses in Venice are the taste of deluded connoisseurship while, for those with eyes to see, the Parthenon sculptures are a new and true set of models for free-thinkers (such as Haydon) to appreciate.

right

FRAMED SET OF MINIATURE PLASTER CASTS OF THE PARTHENON FRIEZE BY JOHN HENNING AT BROOMHALL

c. 1816
Height: 48 cm, Width:145 cm, Depth: 6 cm

These framed casts were produced from moulds carved by the Scottish sculptor John Henning between 1816 and 1820. Unlike the framed set acquired by the British Museum in 2008, this one has been cast in one piece.

Image: by kind permission of Lord Elgin.

MINIATURE CASTS OF THE PARTHENON FRIEZE

Celeste Farge, MA and Alex Truscott, BA

The Department of Greece and Rome at the British Museum holds a set of exquisitely carved slate moulds, reproducing in miniature, the Ionic frieze of the Parthenon. They are one of the finest legacies of the Scottish miniaturist and sculptor John Henning (1771–1851). Born in Paisley, Henning began working for his father, a carpenter, from the age of thirteen. As a young man he developed an interest in sculpture and began to model portrait medallions.

In 1811, on a visit to London, Henning was urged by a friend to go and see the 'Elgin Marbles', brought to England by Lord Elgin, and which at the time were housed in a temporary museum on the corner of Piccadilly and Park Lane. His profound admiration for the Parthenon Sculptures prompted him to apply for permission from Lord Elgin to draw and model from them. Henning's direct approach to Lord Elgin led him to be one of the first artists to gain access to the sculptures, along with Benjamin West, Benjamin Robert Haydon and Charles Robert Cockerell.

Although Henning hoped to improve his artistic skill by studying the sculptures, it is clear from a letter to Josiah Wedgwood in 1813 that he was also looking for a way of supporting his growing family. Encouraged by the 18th and 19th century taste for Classical sculpture and their casts, plus the interest sparked by the arrival of the 'Elgin Marbles' in England, Henning hoped that his work on the sculptures would benefit him financially.

In 1816, Henning tried to get Josiah Wedgwood interested in manufacturing his casts of the Parthenon frieze, in the belief that the popularity of the casts would increase if sold by a well-known company. Writing to Wedgwood, Henning expressed his wish to send him some of the impressions of his ivory carvings of the frieze. Sometime after this, Henning thought of creating a mould by carving intaglio into slate.

When the 'Elgin Marbles' were purchased for the British Museum, with a grant voted by Parliament in 1816, Henning continued to study them in the galleries and was granted permission by the Principal Librarian Henry Ellis to sell his drawings of them. In all, Henning spent 12 years drawing and studying the sculptures and working out the order of the figures of the frieze. In an advertisement of 1820, he stated that his aim was to reproduce the Parthenon frieze as faithfully as possible and to restore the fragmentary areas in the same character. Writing to a friend in 1847, Henning mentioned that he had consulted reproductions of drawings by Jacques Carrey, an artist employed by the Marquis Olier de Nointel, French ambassador to Ottoman Constantinople. Dating from 1674, Carrey's drawings are the only accurate record of the Parthenon sculptures before the explosion of 1687, which caused extensive damage to the building. Henning found Carrey's drawings lacking in detail but they proved invaluable, enabling him to establish an order of the procession in the frieze. Henning's order is not consistent with that preferred today, worked out by Dr Ian

Bibliography

- Jenkins, I. (1994) *The Parthenon Frieze*. London: British Museum Press
- Jenkins, I. (2005) 'The Parthenon frieze and Perikles' cavalry of a thousand', in Barringer, J. and Hurwit, J. (eds.) *Periklean Athens and its Legacy* : University of Texas Press, pp.147–161

- Malden, J. (1977) *John Henning 1771–1851: '...a very ingenious modeller'*. Paisley: Renfrew Museum and Art Gallery
- Wall, J. (2008) *That Most Ingenious Modeller: The Life and Works of John Henning, Sculptor 1771–1851*. Ely

Jenkins of the British Museum in 1994 and now restored as the accepted arrangement in both the British and Acropolis Museums. Jenkins himself readily acknowledges Henning's ingenuity to resolve the problem of how the cavalcade of the south and north long friezes were accommodated, for in each long side there are 60 riders carved into a depth of stone which is never more than 7 cm. It was in facing the same problem as the ancient carvers that Henning had to rediscover their original solution, as was acknowledged by the first 19th century scholar to write on the problem, William Watkiss Lloyd.

Other possible sources that Henning may have used for his restorations include drawings by Feodor Ivanovitch, who was employed by Lord Elgin to make on the-spot-records of the sculptural decoration. The British Museum acquired these drawings along with the 'Elgin Marbles' in 1816.

Henning finally carved 37 individual moulds replicating the Parthenon frieze at one-twentieth of the original size, measuring between 5.7 cm and 6.2 cm in height and varying between 11.8 cm and 32.3 cm in length. The dates on these moulds range from 1816 to 1820. Casts from the moulds were advertised by Henning in 1820 as complete sets framed in root of oak and glazed, or fitted up in six cases in imitation of volumes, for £31 10s. They were also available in mahogany cabinets containing nine drawers, or framed in decorative woods such as the splendid set in Morocco and root of oak purchased by George IV for £42 in 1821.

Henning's miniature casts proved so popular that pirated copies were being sold throughout Europe. By 1835 a French firm was boasting sales of 6,000 copies of Henning's casts. This not only ruined Henning financially but also caused him additional distress because many of them were inferior in quality. In 1837 Henning harangued a Mr J. G. Grace in the Elgin Room of the British Museum for buying pirated casts in the gallery and complained that the custodian on duty did nothing to prevent the sale. As a result of the wide availability of pirated copies, Henning was forced several times to reduce the price of his casts. In 1830 he reduced a set of Parthenon and Bassae casts without frames from £33 10s to £8 and those framed in satinwood and glazed from £42 to £16 16s, while later in 1841 he reduced the price even further to one-fourth of the original cost.

John Henning, while not widely known today, was recognised in his own lifetime. He exhibited at the Royal Academy in the 1820s, and at various times at the British Institution and the Royal Scottish Academy. Henning's miniature casts can be found in many public and private collections, including the Fitzwilliam Museum in Cambridge, and the framed set in this exhibition belonging to Lord Elgin. ∎

Image: by kind permission of Lord Elgin.

DRAWINGS BY JOHN HENNING OF THE PARTHENON FRIEZE AND TWO FIGURES FROM THE PEDIMENTS

Professor Elizabeth A. Moignard, MA DPhil FSA FRSE,
Classics, University of Glasgow

The drawings by John Henning are selected from Lord Elgin's private portfolio, which is still in the family possession at Broomhall; they were made from casts and drawings of the sculptures made in Athens for the 7th Earl of Elgin at the time of their acquisition, as well as from the originals actually transported to London. Henning gained permission to make drawings in their second site at Burlington House in 1811, and continued to draw them after their final arrival in the British Museum in 1817. At that time the original parts of the frieze were displayed with casts of the sections which remained in Athens; the west frieze remained on the building until 1993. Henning also had access to Jacques Carrey's drawings of the sculptures, made in 1674, which show the sculptures before an explosion that damaged them and the building severely in 1687. Further information was available to him from drawings by William Pars and from Stuart and Revett's *Antiquities of Athens**. Henning's drawings demonstrate an interest in the light, shade and curvature of the reliefs, and their effects are perhaps softer than those of his predecessors.

All but one of the drawings exhibited here are of slabs from the west frieze of the Parthenon, much of which remained on the building until it was taken down in the major restoration and cleaning operation of the early 1990s. The frieze shows a procession, usually associated with the central ceremony in the major celebration of civic identity of Classical Athens, the Panathenaia. The procession made its way along the major arterial road across the city centre to the Acropolis, where it fulfilled its primary purpose of sacrifice and the presentation of a newly-woven robe to Athena, the city's patron goddess. As the viewer follows the frieze around the Parthenon from arrival at the west end, it presents the rear section of the procession as a cavalcade, preparing on the west face of the temple, and then moving with increasing vigour along the long north and south sides, where it follows chariots with armed performers leaping in and out of them. Ahead of the cavalcade, about two-thirds of the way along the long faces of the building, the viewer then sees the pedestrian section of the ceremonial: elders, musicians, figures carrying sacred vessels, and the sacrificial cattle and sheep. As the north and south friezes turn the corners onto the east face, the procession then shows the female participants, some of whom are probably carrying the components of the loom on which they have woven the new robe, and the heroes who represent the ten political tribes of Athens. They frame the Olympian gods, themselves seated

* Stuart, J.& Revett, N. (1762-1816) *The antiquities of Athens and other monuments of Greece*. London.

on either side of a central tableau, which is usually read as the presentation and reception of the new robe; the tableau is placed above the central gap between the columns of the temple through which the viewer would see the temple's main entrance door, and the gold and ivory statue of Athena.

The presentation of the Panathenaic procession here is in some sense idealised, as the presence of the gods indicates. In reality, according to contemporary accounts, it was a pedestrian event. The emphasis on cavalry in this image is a matter of ongoing debate about its significance. One very influential interpretation made the frieze a war memorial for the battle of Marathon, viewed as an iconic establisher of Athenian civic identity: the men who fought and died there had just taken part in the Panathenaic festival. The frequent nudity and the association with the horse are indicators of heroic status. A more recent suggestion links the sculptured cavalry with a new emphasis on its real-life importance in the Athens of Pericles' day, in which he sought to enhance its status and numbers, and clarify its organisation against the background of what was to prove to be a long and debilitating interstate war. The Panathenaic festival included competitive sport, for which prizes of high-grade oil in specialised jars

were awarded. Equestrian events involving horses, and some with chariots were a part of the games from very early in their established history, and we may be seeing a reflection of both competition and military priorities in the frieze cavalcade.

The west frieze is composed of rectangular blocks which are rather longer than many of their counterparts on the north and south sides, and the reliefs carved on them tend to remain contained within the edges of their block, rather than overlapping onto its neighbour. Although they work, from the south-west corner of the building, as the start of a moving cavalcade collecting itself to follow the ranks ahead, these reliefs are also easily read as a series of groups involving one or two horses and their riders with more static studies of other human contributors to the scene. Both horses and men are depicted with evident observation of behaviour and posture, which contributes strongly to the ethos of the drawings of them shown in this exhibition: they become highly successful single studies, and credible pieces of flat art. The dramatic qualities of these scenes were clearly a central interest for the draughtsman, and they place a marked emphasis on the horses' heads, and the physical articulation and stance of both horses and men. ∎

Image: by kind permission of Lord Elgin.

WEST XIII

Graphite
Dimensions: Height: 273 mm, Width: 375 mm
Frame approx: Height: 460 mm, Width: 520 mm

The original slab is now very worn, and particularly severely abraded horizontally across its centre, though the upper part of the man and the head of the nearer horse remain relatively clear. Elgin's cast of 1802 shows rather more of the central section, though still damaged. Henning's drawing restores much of what is missing, on the basis of the cast. It emphasises the open, neighing mouth as the horse rears; the drawing shows us the pawing forelegs, now missing. The man is central to the composition, concentrating on restraining the further horse; his head is bent, the face parallel to that of the horse he controls, leaning back, feet well apart to pull on the reins. He has a wide-brimmed hat, similar to that worn by one of the figures on West IX, here slung on his back over his cloak, which Henning shows swinging out behind the rearing forelegs of the second horse, creating a sharply spiked focus to the composition. The slab West XIV, to the right of this one, has two men restraining another horse rearing in the opposite direction; it is not quite a mirror image of this one, but it is as dramatic in its composition and the poses taken by its figures.

Images: by kind permission of Lord Elgin.

WEST XII

Fine black chalk on rag paper toned to various shades with watercolour wash
Dimensions: Height: 202 mm, Width: 282 mm

The original slab is still one of the best-preserved slabs from the southern end of the west frieze, and Henning's drawing suggests that he was seeing the principal sculptures very much as we see them today. The bottom right corner of the slab has gone, and some other drawings of the relief duly tidy the composition by removing the boy standing beside the horse's rump. The remaining scene is one of the most attractive of the west frieze: it centres on the elegant curve of the horse's neck as it rubs its nose on its front left fetlock, the right leg extended behind the neck to provide a triangular focus at the centre of the group. The drawing places more emphasis on the horse's eye and its surrounding facial structure than the now worn original does, and it pays less attention to the texture of the horse's mane, where the sculpture balances its sharp incision with the fine folds and pleats of the *chiton* worn by the figure at the right of the group. The two men are posed as mirror images in *contrapposto*, the further leg supporting the stance, and the nearer one extended with the foot turned outwards – an almost balletic pose which appears elsewhere on the frieze, though perhaps in less exaggerated form. Here the hip above the supporting leg protrudes sharply, with a corresponding deep inward curve on the other side. The man on the right turns towards his companion, and raises his right arm in a commanding wave. The hand is vertically above the horse's head, and leads the eye back to it. His companion, who is naked except for a cloak tied at the base of his neck, looks downwards towards the horse's head, and holds his right arm across his waist. The drawing emphasises the musculature of both figures, and echoes the strong articulation between the parts of the body shown by the relief. The relief suggests a comfortable relationship between men and horse, which this drawing reflects carefully, recognising the compositional focus which draws the attention back to the horse.

top

WEST X

Fine black chalk on rag paper toned to various shades with watercolour wash
Dimensions: Height: 201 mm, Width: 282 mm

The horses and their riders are now moving, and the series of studies that follow show paired or single riders, moving right to left, towards the north-west corner of the building. Here, as on the other compositions with two horses, they are overlapped, with the further rider ahead, in such a way that both riders are visible, and the heads of both horses can be shown to advantage. The cavalry shown later on the frieze represent a series of ranks, some as many as eight deep, which involves close packing on each relief slab. Here they are more relaxed and spaced, as the drawing shows. The nearer horse rears back onto his hind legs and neighs: his booted rider leans with him, his cloak flaring behind him, and holds onto the now missing browband and reins, which were bronze additions. The drawing does not attempt to restore them, but emphasizes the horse's open mouth – we can hear the noise. The further rider is naked above the waist, and both relief and drawing round the shoulders and incline the head as he concentrates on control of the horse and keeping his muzzle down. Again, the drawing places more emphasis on the open mouth than its original. Both show the upper contour of the group as an arch, with the apex at the nose of the nearer horse. His rider's flaring cloak will be repeated, with variations, to suggest rapid movement.

Images: by kind permission of Lord Elgin.

bottom

WEST IX

Fine black chalk on rag paper toned to various shades with watercolour wash
Dimensions: Height: 200 mm, Width: 283 mm

This study again shows a pair of riders, moving forwards more purposefully than those on West X. The nearer horse is trying to force the pace, but is closely restrained by his rider, who brings his head down firmly. The drawing emphasises the pressure around the horse's eyes and muzzle, and the sureness of his rider's controlling hand. The rider wears a *chiton* and a cloak, which remain close to his body, perhaps to suggest a slower movement. He also wears a traveller's hat, which is now very worn on the original relief; the drawing shows its distinctive brim clearly. The rear legs of the horse were evidently already missing; the drawing restores them, and the further horse's tail, as a ghostly outline – a principled compromise between reportage and outright restoration. The further horse stalls slightly on his left foreleg, the right front leg raised in an acute angle. He whinnies, making strong wrinkles around his mouth, and his ears are flattened back on his head. His rider is dressed in *chiton* and cloak, like his companion, and is exercising firm control on the horse. His head is now largely lost: the drawing shows that he was bare-headed, and a fold of his cloak was flying out behind his neck, marking the highest point of the composition.

top

WEST VII

Fine black chalk on rag paper toned to various
shades with watercolour wash
Dimensions: Height: 201 mm, Width: 278 mm

This slab shows a single rider who has not yet mounted his
excited horse. The scene is full of movement, horse, man,
and his clothing, fanned out across the space. The horse rears
noisily, neck arched back, nose horizontal and front legs
flailing. His rider, leans back in a strong diagonal, trying to
control him, throwing out his left arm behind him, echoing
the floating waves of his cloak, which fill the space to the
right of the group, and emphasise the speed and energy of
the pair. Compositionally, the arm and cloak balance the
horse's front legs, and form the supporting struts of an
inverted fan-shape. The rider's face is now lost; the drawing
shows us that he was bearded, unlike most of the riders on
the frieze, and was wearing a close-fitting cap with a flying
tail. One other such figure is shown, mounted, on West IV
(not in the exhibition); the two men may represent the senior
officers, or hipparchs. This slab was virtually in the centre of
the west frieze, and provides a strong punctuation element in
its overall structure.

bottom

WEST V

Fine black chalk on rag paper toned to various
shades with watercolour wash
Dimensions: Height: 202 mm, Width: 295 mm

This study shows two cavalrymen, one already dressed
and mounted, the other naked but for his cloak, standing
by his horse, holding the reins. The mounted figure, is in
many ways, a quieter version of the figures already seen in
slabs IX and X, riding a slightly calmer horse, though still
moving and whinnying. The rider's clothing remains close
to his body and he is sitting comfortably. The standing
figure is another splendid *contrapposto* study, showing a less
exaggerated curvature than his companions on slab XII, but
much the same attention to the torso and leg musculature.
His face is now lost: the drawing suggests that he was looking
towards his mounted colleague. His horse, like that of his
companion, is paying attention to the riders on slab IV (not
in the exhibition). As ever, the drawing places emphasis on
the contours of the figures and their anatomical details, to
give us a strong sense of their volume and of the apparent
depth of the relief.

Images: by kind permission of Lord Elgin.

top

WEST III

Fine black chalk on rag paper toned to various
shades with watercolour wash
Dimensions: Height: 202 mm, Width: 288 mm

This is a group of three men with a horse. The figure beside
the horse's head is usually interpreted as its owner; he is
another *contrapposto* study, naked but for a cloak fastened
around his neck, very like his equivalents on slabs V and
XII. He looks away to the left towards the figures on slab
II; he is presented frontally, but lifts his hands to the horse's
nose, which brings his right arm across his body. The horse
responds, mouth slightly open, ears back, and hind legs bent
a little. At his rump stands a boy, acting as his groom, talking
to the third figure, a bearded marshal, who passes behind
the horse, gesturing toward the front of the procession, head
turned back to speak to him. The drawing again foregrounds
the figure contours, especially those of the horse, and plays
down the garments. The face of the figure on the left was
evidently largely worn at the time of the casting: its outline
is there, but the drawing shades its detail away. The marshal's
lower face is now very worn; the drawing shows us his profile
and mouth. The groom, in profile, with right leg crossed
over left and hands across his chest, is better preserved, and
the drawing gives a certain emphasis to the conversation in
which the two are engaged.

Images: by kind permission of Lord Elgin.

bottom

WEST II

Fine black chalk on rag paper toned to various
shades with watercolour wash
Dimensions: Height: 203 mm, Width: 346 mm

This slab, with its two riders, is in the British Museum. It fits
next to the turn into the north side, where the cavalcade sets
off in earnest. To the left of our first horseman, carved on
the return of the first block of the north face, was a marshal,
marking the corner and guiding the riders towards it. Both
horses move forwards energetically: the leader has his ears
turned forwards, and leads the way; the second appears more
nervous, ears back, head raised, and nostrils distended, a
detail noted strongly in the drawing. This may be partially
a reaction to the rider of the first horse, who turns to
gesture with his left arm sharply up. He has a dismounted
twin on the next slab round the corner, North XLII (not
in the exhibition) – another fine nude study, making the
same gesture, hand to head. The second rider here is seen in
profile, leaning back in tune with his horse as it rears.

right

NORTH XXXVI

Fine black chalk on rag paper toned to various shades with watercolour wash
Dimensions: Height: 203 mm, Width: 244 mm

This slab comes from the centre of the galloping cavalcade. The slab was split, and the drawing shows only half of the slab. To the right of the drawing we see a neighing head, raised front legs, and part of a rider. The rest of both the horse and the man are on the other half of the slab. There are two other horses carrying their men speedily forwards. The drawing strongly emphasises the horses' legs, so that the technical expertise with which the multiple overlap suggests the dense ranking is foregrounded here, as is the graphic quality of the carving.

Image: by kind permission of Lord Elgin.

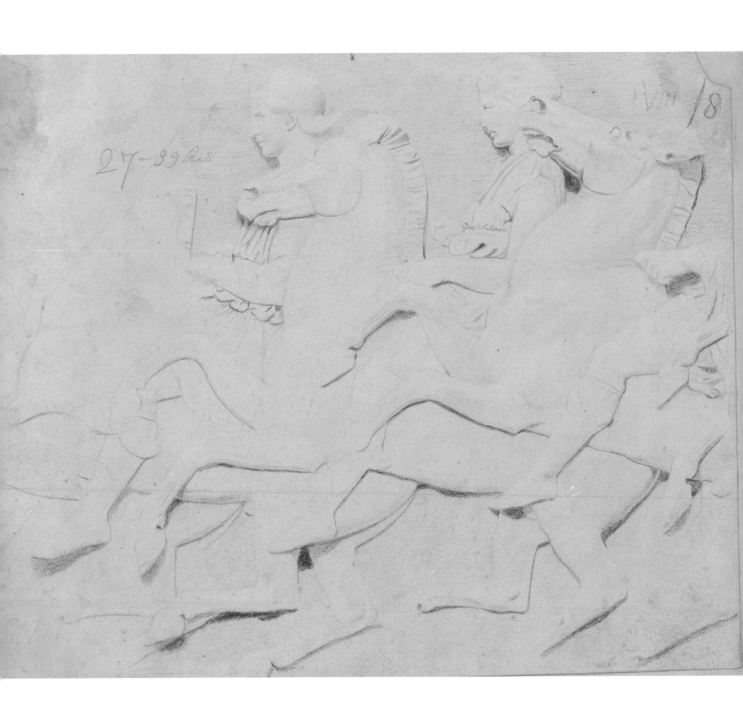

top

WEST PEDIMENT A

Fine black chalk on rag paper toned to various
shades with watercolour wash
Dimensions: Height: 231 mm, Width: 321 mm

The west pediment of the Parthenon, the first that the visitor to the Acropolis saw, showed the competition between the patron goddess Athena, and her uncle Poseidon, the sea god, for Athens and its territory and people. This is a foundation myth which reflects on the presence of cults of both deities on the Acropolis, and on the importance of both their spheres of influence for the well-being of the Athenian state. As the story goes, Athena offered the people of Athens, who were watching the contest, the olive; Poseidon countered by striking the rock of the Acropolis with his trident and releasing a fountain of sea-water. The mark of his trident was visible, preserved beneath the floor of the north porch of the Erechtheion, just across the processional path from the Parthenon. Athena's olive stood in the enclosed garden nearby.

The pedimental sculptures grouped the two gods as a powerful, fighting v-shape in the centre, and then framed them with their chariots, and groups of seated or reclining local gods and heroes, not all easily identified. The figure in West A, the subject of this drawing, is usually identified as a god representing one of the local rivers, the Ilissos; the corresponding figure at the other end, also reclining into the corner of the pediment, is usually identified as another.

The drawing shows the figure viewed from the front, which emphasises the boat-like curvature of the body and the raised leg. As often, Henning shows more interest in the articulation of the rib-cage and the musculature than in the cloak draped over the god's left arm, on which he props himself up. In reality, the cloak can also be read as the river water, and it loops along the length of the figure's back in an undulating swag. The drawing reflects the fact that, in situ, the back of the figure was not visible.

bottom

EAST PEDIMENT D

Fine black chalk on rag paper toned to various
shades with watercolour wash
Dimensions: Height: 231 mm, Width: 311 mm

The east pediment of the Parthenon showed the other major cult legend, the Birth of Athena, who sprung fully armed from her father Zeus' head. The event was usually shown as witnessed by the other Olympians, and this was the case here, as with the reception of the peplos on the section of the frieze below. Athena stands greeting an enthroned Zeus in the centre of the pediment, and the witnesses move, sit or recline on either side of the central group. At the extreme ends of the pediment are the chariots of the rising sun and the setting moon, Selene. The head of her horse is one of the enduring masterpieces of sculpture from the Parthenon. Lord Elgin's cast of it appears elsewhere in the exhibition, as do drawings of it by Benjamin Robert Haydon.

The figure in East D, reclining on an animal skin, is usually identified as the god of wine, Dionysos. His posture is that assumed by drinkers at a symposion; the missing hand probably held a cup. The sculpture is one of the few which survives with its head intact, short-haired and soft-featured. The drawing restores the damage to the nose and the left side of the face. It also reflects a certain physical flabbiness which has suggested the alcoholic preoccupations of the god, and their effects. This figure also appears prominently (as does West A), in the Cockerell drawing of the temporary exhibition shown here and in Haydon's version, both of which foreground the quasi-freestanding sculptures from the Parthenon rather than the reliefs.

Images: by kind permission of Lord Elgin.

right

A DRAWING OF THE TEMPORARY ELGIN ROOM BY CHARLES ROBERT COCKERELL

1807
Black ink
Dimensions: Height: 420 mm, Width: 620 mm
Frame: Height: 620 mm, Width: 790 mm

The marbles acquired by Lord Elgin were first displayed to the public in London in 1807-1811 in a temporary exhibition space in Park Lane. They were acquired for the nation in 1816 after a Parliamentary Select Committee investigated the prospect, and went on display in the Temporary Elgin Room recorded in Archibald Archer's painting.*

Charles Robert Cockerell, later famous as the architect of the Ashmolean Museum in Oxford and other neo-classical buildings, is also remembered as an archaeologist who investigated and recorded surviving ruins in Greece. He helped to excavate the temple of Aphaia on Aegina in 1811, and recorded the temple of Apollo at Bassae. His reconstruction of the interior of the Temple of Apollo, with the first known Corinthian column, is still much-illustrated. He acquired its frieze, which is now in the British Museum. He used and adapted the architecture and decoration of this temple in his design for the Ashmolean. In April 1810, Cockerell left for the tour which gave him these opportunities; he was given an introduction to the artist Lusieri, then acting as Lord Elgin's agent, in the form of a note from the then Under Secretary of State for Foreign Affairs which was written on the back of a more elaborate version of the sketch in this exhibition:

'My dear friend,
   Take this in remembrance of one who often thinks of you and wishes to see you here, and in recommendation of The Bearer my particular Friend Mr. C.R. Cockerell, who has made the drawing to show you how we prize in London the Relicks of The Parthenon'   W. Hamilton

That sketch remained in Cockerell's possession, and that of his descendants, and appears as Fig.10 in an article by P. Hunt and A.H. Smith.**

The drawing exhibited here, which looks like an earlier draft, shows the marbles disposed around the edges of the temporary shed to create a viewing space in the centre. Sections of the architrave of the Erechtheion act as hedges at the front of the drawing; the single Caryatid from the south porch stands in the centre of the further range. Frieze sections from the Parthenon and the temple of Athena Nike, and the Parthenon *metopes* are arranged as effectively continuous strips along the outer walls, as background, beyond figures from the Parthenon pediments, which are mainly displayed as single sculptures on low plinths on the floor. The Caryatid is flanked by the seated female figure K and the standing figure G, both from the east pediment, and both detached from their original neighbours. Figures L and M, which were next to K on the building, are displayed at the right, on the other side of the reclining D. Figure A from the west pediment provides a balance to the left of figure K. Figures E and F from the east pediment balance their counterparts L and M on the left of the space, with figure H from the west pediment in the foreground, on a pedestal formed from a memorial stone to Aristeides, son of Lysimachos. Opposite is a column from the Erechtheion, still with its neck-ring and *echinus*, which has been pressed into service as a plinth for the head of Selene's horse from the north corner of the east pediment.

Perhaps the most significant observation recorded here is the firm dissociation of the sculptures from the building; they are displayed as works of art to be viewed independently of their architectural framework and compositional raison d'être. The pedimental triangle which underpins the relationships and placing of figures and groups has been abandoned in favour of a display which focuses on their separate qualities, though still largely those which are appreciated from the front.

---

* Archibald Archer (1819) '*The Temporary Elgin Room*', British Museum. (Not in the exhibition)
** Hunt, P. & Smith, A.H. (1916) 'Lord Elgin and his Collection', *Journal of Hellenic Studies,* 36, p.299.

Image: by kind permission of Lord Elgin.

West H

Caryatid

Selene's horse
on Erechtheion
column

East E
and F

West A

East K

East G

East D

East L
and M

left

A VIEW OF THE PARK LANE DISPLAY
BY BENJAMIN ROBERT HAYDON, 1808

Black and white chalks on brown paper
Dimensions: Height: 460 mm, Width: 640 mm
Frame: Height: 690 mm, Width: 840 mm

Haydon was one of the foremost artists and critics in the establishment of the Parthenon sculptures as the gold standard against which to measure Classical Greek art – perhaps the first to grasp their significance and to establish a sense of their relationship to other antique sculptures. He received permission to draw the sculptures in the display in Park Lane in the spring of 1808, and continued to do so until the early summer of 1813. He took the poet John Keats to see them, and conveyed a view of them as markers of the simplicity and fidelity to nature which are the key principles of Greek art; this found its way into Keats' poetry and working ethos. Haydon's autobiography gives a graphic account of his continuing fascination with the 'Marbles':

'I had been contemplating what Socrates looked at and Plato saw'; he evidently treated the Park Lane display as a personal learning space at an important stage of his career, studying and drawing over extended periods. Many of his drawings and their details formed the basis of figures in his paintings of other subjects; in a letter to Lord Elgin in 1809 he expresses a continuing fascination with 'the Horse's head, the reclining figure, and the Theseus with the two sitting, the two lying Women'. He says that these are 'quite enough to reform Art or create it, wherever they appear'.

This drawing shows the display from behind the reclining figure, (east pediment D) identified by Haydon and his contemporaries as Theseus, now usually thought of as Dionysos, down the right side of the room as shown in the Cockerell drawing (previous page); we see the adjoining end of the pedimental group L and M, and some of the architectural fragments beyond. The focus of the study is the vigorous musculature of the reclining god's back, drawn, characteristically of Haydon, as though from a living model rather than from a marble. He describes his reaction to this sculpture and that of the river god (west pediment A) in his autobiography:

'But when I turned to the Theseus, and saw that every form was altered by action or repose, - when I saw that the two sides of his back varied, one side stretched from the shoulder blade being pushed close to the spine, as he rested on his elbow, with the belly flat because the bowels fell into the pelvis as he sat, - and when, turning to the Ilyssus, I saw the belly protruded, from the figure lying on its side … when I saw, in fact, the most heroic style of art, combined with all the essential detail of actual life, the thing was done at once and for ever.

Here were principles which the commonsense of the English people would understand; here were principles which the great Greeks in their finest time established …

… all night I dozed and dreamed of the marbles. I rose at five in a fever of excitement, tried to sketch the Theseus from memory, did so, and saw that I comprehended it. At last I got an order for myself; I rushed away to Park Lane; the impression was more vivid than before.'

Image: by kind permission of Lord Elgin.

left

STUDIES OF SELENE'S HORSE
BY BENJAMIN ROBERT HAYDON

Graphite
Dimensions: Height: 292 mm, Width: 384 mm
Frame approx: Height: 460 mm, Width: 520 mm

The central action of the east pediment of the Parthenon is framed by the chariots of the Sun (Helios) and Moon (Selene), which rise and set in the corners, a brilliant solution to the compositional problem posed by the narrowing lateral points of the triangle. The heads of Selene's chariot horses appear above the floor of the pediment, fanning and overlapping, with the furthest head in profile with its muzzle in the angle. The head of the nearest horse is angled out over the edge of the pedimental frame, and remains a magnificent three-dimensional study: it is one of the best-preserved sculptures of the set. It was clearly a major catalyst of admiration and interest to Haydon, who drew it several times, with varying degrees of interpretation. Its fidelity to observed equine characteristics was a particular concern: many of the studies are foregrounding the adrenaline-charged and exhausted working animal of real life which lies behind the Moon's declining trace-horse. The four studies here restore and emphasise muscular details and angularities which have been smoothed by time and wear in the original sculpture, as the cast in this exhibition shows. Haydon's drawings use his control of line to show us the stretch of the returned ears, the bulging eyes, the distended nostrils and the panting mouth. There is a strong feeling for both the animal and the drama of its sculptural interpretation. These studies, and the other versions in the exhibition are among Haydon's most moving and exciting drawings.

Image: by kind permission of Lord Elgin.

right

DRAWING BY HENNING OF A METOPE FROM THE TEMPLE OF HEPHAISTOS IN THE ATHENIAN AGORA

Black chalk
Dimensions: Height: 317 mm, Width: 308 mm
Frame approx: Height: 460 mm, Width: 520 mm

The temple of Hephaistos, sometimes known as the Thesion stands on a low hill overlooking the Athenian *Agora*, and is one of the better-preserved examples of architecture from the 5th century BC. Much of its metope and frieze sculpture remained on the building, and was drawn both for Stuart and Revett and later for Lord Elgin, who also had casts made. Not all the metopes on the building had sculptures, unlike those of the Parthenon; the sculptures come from the east end of the building, running round its corners to extend for a short distance along the north and south sides. The east metopes show the Labours of Herakles, and the four on each of the north and south sides show the adventures of Theseus. Both sets of adventures are presented as individual groups of hero and opponent. Henning's drawing shows North *metope* 4, which depicts Theseus confronting and attacking a fallen figure;

South *metope* 1 does too, which has led to difficulties in identifying his opponent. The likely candidates are the giant Prokrustes and Hephaistos' son Periphetes. Henning's drawing records the state of the relief which was found by Elgin's cast-makers: the hero's arms are lost apart from the hand across his chest, which is usually reconstructed as holding the shank of an axe. The right arm can be reconstructed from the remaining muscles at the shoulder as raised to grasp the axe near the head to bring it down on the fallen figure, who held out his hands in a powerful pleading gesture. The arms of both figures created a strong, violent diagonal across the centre of the panel powerfully suggested by the gap in Henning's drawing. He makes no attempt at restoration here, and the emphasis of the drawing is very much on the musculature of both figures, especially Theseus' powerful frontal torso and the overlapping legs.

Image: by kind permission of Lord Elgin.

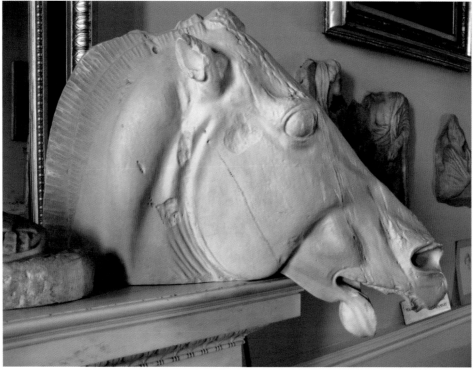

left

CAST OF SELENE'S HORSE

British Musem cast
Dimensions: Height: 64 cm, Width: 84 cm, Depth: 26 cm

The east pediment of the Parthenon depicts the birth of Athena from the head of Zeus, witnessed by the other Olympian gods. A visitor would have moved round the building from the west end to reach the point of entry to the building, with its gold and ivory cult statue of the goddess. The east end of the frieze, above the door, shows the culminating part of the procession, the hand-over of the new peplos, witnessed by the gods. The metopes on this end of the building show the gods, probably including the Sun and Moon, fighting the giants. Altogether there was strong emphasis on the divine and related phenomena at this end of the temple. Athena and her father were in the centre of the low triangle formed by the gable end of the temple, dominating the composition. On either side were moving and reclining gods, including Dionysos seen in several of the drawings in the exhibition,

and the event is given an element of time and space by the presence of the chariots of the rising Sun in the left corner, and the setting Moon in the right. The fanned and layered horses' heads of the Moon's Selene's chariot team fit into and splay out of the low corner of the pediment; this head, of the near trace-horse, protruded over the edge of the pediment floor. It is a powerful representation of the horse as a competitive, excited animal: stressed, panting, hard-worked. The sculpture demonstrates the same powers of observation and understanding of the horse that we find in those on the frieze – a major factor in its popularity at the time of its first appearance in the Park Lane display, and now in the Duveen Gallery in The British Museum. It has an intensely sympathetic and tactile quality, despite its original siting on an inaccessible part of the building it adorned.

Images: by kind permission of Lord Elgin.

right

CAST OF THE ELGIN THRONE

Resin cast made from the original which was a gift from the Archbishop of Athens to Thomas, Earl of Elgin in 1802
Dimensions: Height: 80 cm, Width: 69 cm, Depth: 71 cm

The marble throne from which this was cast was originally a formal seat in a public space in Athens, possibly the Theatre of Dionysos, for the holder of an important public office. It dates from the 4th century BC. The original was once in the Elgin collection, and is now in the Getty Museum, Malibu. The throne has two narrative reliefs with a specifically Athenian reference: one shows the Tyrant Slayers, Harmodios and Aristogeiton, and the other Theseus and the Amazon. Harmodios and Aristogeiton were celebrated in Athens as heroes of the democracy; their statues stood in the *Agora* on a site protected from encroaching rivals by law. The first set of reliefs, installed not long after the assassination which gave rise to the legend, were stolen by the Persians in the invasion of 480 BC, and were replaced by the second set, by Kritios and Nesiotes, very quickly once the invasion was over. Alexander the Great restored the original set when he re-captured them on sacking Susa. The second group are represented in contemporary vase-paintings and sculptural reliefs: they were a symbol of an important strand in the Athenian sense of identity, which is why they appear in this exhibition in an official civic context. Theseus, the legendary Athenian king, appears frequently in Athenian art of the Classical era: he, too, is an important expression of the Athenian sense of identity. His defence of Athens against the invading Amazons appears often in the city's sculpture. The Parthenon and the Hephaisteion both have representations of the fight: the West *Metopes* of the Parthenon dominate the viewer's first sight of the building on the spot where the fight notionally happened.

Image: by kind permission of Lord Elgin.

OUR GRATITUDE TO:

Professor Elizabeth A Moignard,
MA DPhil FSA FRSE, Classics
University of Glasgow, Author and Scholarly Researcher

Dr Ian Jenkins, OBE FSA, Senior Curator,
Department of Greece and Rome, The British Museum

The Earl of Elgin and Kincardine, KT,
Author and Loans

Mr Neil MacGregor, OM, Director, The British Museum

Dr Andrew Burnett, Deputy Director, The British Museum

John Orna Ornstein,
Head of London and National Programmes,
The British Museum

Lesley Fitton, Keeper,
Department of Greece and Rome, The British Museum

Hugo Chapman, Keeper,
Department of Prints and Drawings, The British Museum

Celeste Farge, MA, Curator of Drawings
Department of Greece and Rome, The British Museum

Alex Truscott, BA, Senior Museum Assistant
Department of Greece and Rome, The British Museum

Trevor Coughlan, Senior Administrator,
Department of Greece and Rome, The British Museum

Andrew Bashan, Senior Administrator and Loans Registrar,
Prints and Drawings, The British Museum

Scottish Conservation Studio, Hopetoun

THE MORAY ART CENTRE TEAM:

Randy Klinger, Founder and Director
Exhibition concept and Premise

Freda Matassa, Exhibition Registrar

Katrin Uecker, Graphic Designer

Diane A. Smith, Centre Manager

Christine Dodwell, Arts Administrator

Gill Bird, Education & Exhibitions Manager

Kresanna Aigner, Arts Events Manger/Volunteer Coordinator,

Helen Beveridge, Marketing and PR Officer

Rebecca J.C. Prentice, Education & Exhibition Assistant

Eesha Brander, Gallery & Facilities Assistant

Pat Miller-Randell, Proofreader

Moray Art Centre Volunteer Team

PARTNERS:

Opportunity Enhancement Trust

Right Lines Productions

Charioteer Theatre

Out Of Darkness

LOTTERY FUNDED

Year of Creative Scotland 2012

ALBA | CHRUTHACHAIL